P9-AFR-619

jB P424i
Italia, Robert
H. Ross Perot

ALLEN COUNTY PUBLIC LIBRARY
FORT WAYNE, INDIANA 46802

You may return this book to any location of
the Allen County Public Library.

DEMCO

Everyone Contributes

H. ROSS PEROT

The Man Who Woke Up America

Bob Italia

Allen County Public Library
900 Webster Street
PO Box 2270
Fort Wayne, IN 46801-2270

Published by Abdo & Daughters, 6535 Cecilia Circle, Edina, Minnesota 55439.

Library bound edition distributed by Rockbottom Books, Pentagon Tower, P.O. Box 36036, Minneapolis, Minnesota 55435.

Copyright ©1993 by Abdo Consulting Group, Inc., Pentagon Tower, P.O. Box 36036, Minneapolis, Minnesota 55435. International copyrights reserved in all countries. No part of this book may be reproduced without written permission from the copyright holder. Printed in the U.S.A.

Edited by Rosemary Wallner

Photo Credits: Bettmann - pgs. 5, 33, 34
                  Black Star - pgs. 6, 8, 12, 23, 27, 29, 38
                  Archive - pgs. 16, 18, 34

Cover Photo: Black Star

Library of Congress Cataloging-in-Publication Data

Italia, Robert, 1955-
      H. Ross Perot : The Man Who Woke up America / written by Bob Italia.
         p.   cm. -- (Everyone Contributes)
      Summary: Presents the life of the outspoken businessman from Texarkana whose 1992 presidential bid altered the face of American politics.
      Includes glossary and index.
      ISBN 1-56239-236-0
      1. Perot, H. Ross, 1930- --Juvenile literature.   2. Presidential candidates--United States--Biography--Juvenile literature.   [1.Perot, H. Ross, 1930-
2. Presidential candidates   3. Businessman.]   I. Title.   II. Series: Italia, Robert, 1955-   Everyone Contributes.
      E840.8.P427I83   1993
      973.928'092--dc20
      [B]   93-3682
                                                          CIP
                                                           AC

Table of Contents

The Perot Factor

At first, the 1992 presidential election seemed like the usual political affair. The Democrats lined up to drive the Republicans from the White House. The Republicans braced themselves for a tough fight against the Democrats.

Suddenly, a man from Texas entered the race. His name was Ross Perot. Without formally declaring his candidacy, Perot whipped up a storm of discontent.

In the early 1990s, the economy was going nowhere. American industry was losing its competitive spirit. People were losing their jobs and going deeper into debt. Politicians in Washington, it seemed, were powerless to correct the problems. And neither President George Bush nor his opponent, Bill Clinton, wanted to talk about solutions.

America was angry. They wanted a man of action, a savior. Ross Perot seemed to be that man. His down-to-earth straight talk and can-do attitude made him a strong alternative. No other independent candidate in modern American history mounted a more serious challenge to the two-party system.

In the end, Ross Perot's bid for the White House fell short. But even though he failed, Perot left his mark. He woke up a sluggish political system. Perot changed the way voters look at independent candidates.

The 1992 Presidential race brought to it
a newcomer, a billionaire businessman, who many
people believed would put America back to work.
His name was H. Ross Perot.

Ross Perot went to Patty Hill School, the only private elementary school in Texarkana. Perot is in the back row, 3rd from the left, white pants and shirt.

The Man from Texarkana

H. Ross Perot (pronounced Per-ROW) was born on June 27, 1930, in Texarkana. The city is located in a ragged corner of Texas near the borders of Arkansas, Oklahoma, and Louisiana. Texarkana has long been known as a hangout for hobos and drifters. Outlaws were drawn to the city because it was easy for them to cross state lines.

Perot's father, Gabriel Ross Perot, was a successful cotton broker and horse trader. His mother, Lulu May, was a homemaker. They named their son Henry Ray, after his mother's father.

Perot considers his father the most significant person in his life. A portly man barely five feet tall, Gabriel Ross taught Perot everything he knew about business. Perot sat for hours in his father's brokerage house and watched him conduct business. Sometimes he drove with his father to horse or cattle auctions. Watching and listening to his father was an education that carried Perot very far in the world.

Perot went to Patty Hill School, the only private elementary school in Texarkana. Tuition was $5 a month. There, Perot not only learned reading, writing, and arithmetic, but he also learned about operas and plays and read classic books. Perot learned to recite the Bible and to dance ballroom style.

Ross Perot's boyhood home in Texarkana, Texas.
He lived here with his parents.

Perot joined the school's accordion band. He was too small to play football, so he took up tennis. Though he was not powerful, Perot became a clever player. When his father joined the local country club, Perot became a lifeguard at the club pool.

What's in a Name?

Before Perot was born, his parents' first son, Gabriel Ross Perot Jr., died of a stomach disorder at age three.

"It broke my parents' heart," said Perot, who was born three years after his brother died. "They adored him, and he died of something that you could fix in 20 minutes today."

The Perots confronted the loss, but their pain never disappeared. Gabriel Ross had lost his firstborn and his namesake. When Perot was 12 years old, his parents took him to the courthouse to change his name.

"They did not want to give me my dad's name because of my older brother's memory," said Perot. "But as I grew older, more and more my dad wanted me to have at least part of his name. But they wanted to make a distinction between my brother and me. It was very important to my dad, and I loved him."

And so, Henry Ray Perot legally had his name changed to Henry Ross. His parents began calling him Ross, just like the brother he never knew.

Shortly afterward, Perot became a Boy Scout. In just 16 months, Perot achieved the highest rank in scouting: Eagle Scout. Usually, a scout works on projects for three to five years to become an Eagle Scout. Fewer than 1 percent of scouts even reach this rank. Perot pushed himself to meet all the requirements. His drive and ambition began to show.

Midshipman Perot

In 1949, nineteen-year-old Perot became a midshipman at the U.S. Naval Academy in Annapolis, Maryland. "They issued me two pairs of shoes," recalled Perot. "I wondered what the other pair was for. This was my first example of government waste."

Perot enjoyed the rigid environment at Annapolis. But the course work was geared toward engineering. Business was Perot's strength, and he received average grades.

Despite his schoolwork problems, Perot became the president of his graduating class in 1953. That same year, he met Margot Birmingham. Birmingham was a sophomore at nearby Goucher College. Perot impressed her with his friendly manner and politeness.

In June 1953, Perot graduated. He thought of joining the Marines but decided on the Navy. He wanted to see the world, and sailing on a Navy ship would give him those experiences.

Perot was assigned to a destroyer, the U.S.S. *Sigourney.* "Nine months later," Perot recalled, "I'd gone all the way around the world."

Despite his journeys, Perot was miserable in the Navy. By 1955, he tried to get released from active duty. "My father was very ill," Perot said. "That's what was driving this. He wanted me to be with him if I could."

Perot was also frustrated with the conditions in the Navy. He expected high operating standards. But he claimed that the Navy was far from excellent. He argued with his captain about the way he ran the ship.

Perot's resignation was turned down. Ten days later, his father suffered a heart attack. Perot rushed to his side. He was there when his father died. "I buried him myself 'cause that's the last thing I could do for him," said Perot.

In the fall of 1955, Perot joined the crew of the U.S.S. *Leyte,* an aircraft carrier. After working as gunnery control officer, Perot became an assistant navigator. The position required Perot to learn to use a computer. Suddenly, he had found his future.

ROSS PEROT

TREASURER

H. Ross Perot's college yearbook picture.

IBM's Top Salesman

Perot and Margot were married in September 1956. The following year, Perot's time in the Navy ended. The Perots went to Dallas, Texas, where Perot began to work for International Business Machines (IBM).

IBM's rigid environment was ideal for Perot, but he was not popular with the other employees. He did not socialize with his fellow sales staff. In fact, Perot was rarely seen in the office. Instead, he spent all his time making sales calls. It did not take him long to become a record-setting salesman. Perot worked hard and saved his money, thinking of the future.

In 1958, the first of the Perots' five children, Henry Ross Jr., was born. Henry was soon followed by Nancy, Suzanne, Carolyn, and Katherine.

Though Perot thrived at IBM, he ran into problems. Management was resentful of the money Perot made. Since he was a top salesman, Perot earned more than his supervisors. Frustrated with the jealousies, Perot thought of starting his own company.

Perot noticed that many of his clients did not know how to run their computers. He suggested that IBM expand their services to help these clients. IBM turned down his proposal.

H. Ross Perot, head of Electronic Data Systems Corp. of Dallas, holds a piece of electronic computer equipment which he designed. It replaced the larger pieces of equipment in the background.

Electronic Data Services

Perot turned the IBM setback into an opportunity. In 1962, he started Electronic Data Services (EDS). The company offered data processing for big businesses.

Perot ran his company like a Navy ship, but he rewarded excellence and loyalty. Many of his early employees became wealthy as EDS succeeded.

On September 12, 1968, shares of stock were offered to anyone who wanted to invest in EDS. Stock was sold at $16.50 per share. Since Perot had 9.5 million shares, he was suddenly worth more than $150 million. When the stock hit its peak a year and a half later, EDS was worth $162.50 per share. Perot's fortune was now almost $1.5 billion.

Around the same time, Perot became involved with the Vietnam War. Perot has never been shy about his dedication to the American military. In 1970, he made a Christmas flight to Southeast Asia with dinners for American prisoners of war (POWs). Though the dinners never reached their destination, Perot returned to Dallas an American hero.

Perot kept his eye on Vietnam, even after the POWs began coming home in 1973. Perot was convinced that some POWs had been left behind. He established his own informal intelligence network. And he or his representatives had 47 meetings with North Vietnamese officials. But the issue was never resolved.

Perot became involved in the Vietnam War. His goal was
to bring back as many prisoners of war as possible.
Here he is refused permission to bring Christmas
presents to American POWs.

To this day, Perot is convinced that the North Vietnamese still hold some American soldiers prisoner.

On Wings of Eagles

At Christmastime 1978, an episode occurred that made Perot famous and made him into an American legend. Two EDS employees had been arrested in Tehran, Iran, and put in jail. No formal charges were pressed. But many believed the two paid bribes to gain EDS a contract to computerize the Iranian social security system.

For an entire week, Perot tried to get his employees out through talking with officials. When that failed, he turned to Lieutenant Colonel Arthur (Bull) Simons. Simons was a retired Green Beret commander who had led a failed attempt to rescue American POWs in 1970.

Perot and Simons drew up a rescue plan. Then Perot assembled a seven-man rescue squad made up of EDS employees, most of whom had military experience. Perot placed the team under Simons' command, and they trained at Perot's lake house outside Dallas.

Perot's attorney discovered the plot and confronted Perot. "You have a mercenary army which is illegal here, in Iran, and in every country the team would pass through," the attorney said. "Ross, they'll be shot. Instead of two innocent employees in jail, you could have eight guilty employees dead."

Ross Perot, left, arranged an American-led commando squad to free two of his employees from an Iranian jail. The two men in the middle were the prisoners and the man on the right is a retired U.S. Army Colonel.

Perot was unphased. He was determined to save his employees. He traveled to Tehran and visited his employees at the prison. That's when he discovered that many soldiers guarded the prison. It would be too difficult for a seven-man team to jump over the wall and free the prisoners.

What happened afterward isn't exactly clear. The official version states that an Iranian EDS employee led a mob that overran the prison and freed the prisoners. But the Iranian government claims that prison guards were simply bribed into letting the prisoners go.

Whatever happened, the mission was a total success. The story of the rescue became a best-selling book *On Wings of Eagles* by popular thriller writer Ken Follett. And a TV miniseries was produced. Perot had become a larger-than-life American hero. He was a courageous and powerful man who scorned bureaucracies and got things done. It was a reputation that would carry him far in the 1992 presidential race.

GM Makes an Offer He Can't Refuse

In 1984, General Motors (GM) Chairman Roger Smith offered to buy EDS from Perot. GM's production was struggling and slow. The company needed to become more efficient. Smith wanted to make GM a high-tech operation, and EDS fit right into his plans.

The deal would make Ross Perot one of the richest men in America. But he would lose control of his company. Still, GM needed EDS. He could help save the struggling automaker.

Perot agreed to sell EDS on June 27, 1984, for $2.55 billion. He also received a huge amount of GM stock. EDS helped GM streamline its operations. But Perot struggled to find a role at GM. He did not like the do-nothing attitude of the Board of Directors and often clashed with Smith.

Finally, Smith had enough of Perot and offered to buy back the GM stock—for $700 million. Perot called the deal obscene, but took the money and left GM.

Perot started another company, Perot Systems, and stole his former clients from EDS. He seemed to have it all—wealth, a happy family, and his own business empire. But he was not completely satisfied. He needed a new challenge—someone or something to save. He had $3 billion in the bank and nothing to do.

The Calling

In November 1991, Perot received a call from John J. Hooker. Hooker was a businessman who had dabbled in Tennessee politics. He wanted Perot to run for president of the United States.

Perot quickly turned him down. He did not feel he could be effective in a political system that he despised. Still, he offered his opinions about what was wrong with the country. The country's budget deficit was too high and out of control, American industry was losing its competitive edge in the world economy. American cities were on the decline. The next president needed to take fast and effective action.

Hooker was impressed with Perot. Hooker knew that the American people were angry with the government. The economy was sluggish. Debt was increasing. People wanted action, but the present government seemed incapable of fixing the problems.

Hooker also knew that someone outside the political scene had a good chance to run successfully as an independent candidate. Perot was tops on the list because of his tough, no-nonsense policies and his reputation for quick and successful action. He also had a lot of money. Like many people, Perot was angry with and suspicious of the government. He was not a politician. He was one of the people. He could be the people's savior.

Hooker convinced Perot to fly to Nashville in February 1992 for a radio interview. Afterward, Perot spoke to a group of Nashville community leaders. Someone asked him if he would run for president. Perot laughed and said, "I'd be a square peg in a round hole."

Then a woman asked him if there were any circumstances under which he would run.

Perot paused, then replied, "I really am not interested in being in public life. If you feel strongly about it, register me in 50 states. If you want to do 50 states, you care that much, fine. Then I don't belong to anybody but you. I would not want to run in any of the existing parties because you'd have to sell out."

Larry King Live

That same month, Hooker asked Perot to appear on "Larry King Live." The talk show, hosted by Larry King, is broadcasted on the CNN cable network. Thousands of people watch the show. Perot, who had been on the show during the 1991 Gulf War, was scheduled to talk about the economy.

"Good evening from Washington," King said, staring into the TV camera. "About a third of the voters in New Hampshire's primary said that they wished somebody else were running, and some undoubtedly have this guy (Perot) in mind." King turned to Perot. "Are you going to run?"

"No," Perot said.

"Flat 'no'?" King said with surprise.

"Getting all caught up in a political process that doesn't work. . .I wouldn't be temperamentally fit for it," replied Perot.

Ross Perot appeared on "Larry King Live." Larry
King asked Perot if he would run for President.
Perot answered "No" unless the people of
the U.S. wanted him to run.

"I know John J. Hooker is strongly urging you to do it," said King.

"Well," Perot replied, "I get a tremendous number of calls and letters." Then he steered the conversation to the economy.

Perot dodged the presidential issue throughout the show. King asked Perot five times in 50 minutes if he was going to run. In the final minutes, King boxed him into the corner.

"By the way," King said, "is there any scenario in which you would run for president?"

Perot hesitated. "Now recognize," he said, "you're listening to a guy that doesn't want to do this. But if you, the people, will on your own register me in 50 states, I'll promise you this: between now and the convention we'll get both parties' heads straight."

Perot returned to his hotel room where his wife was waiting for him. She had watched the show on TV and looked stunned. "I can't believe you did that!" she said. She did not want him running for president.

Perot was not concerned. "It'll never happen," he assured her.

President Perot?

When the Perots returned to Dallas the next morning, the telephone lines were flooded with calls from well-wishers. By the end of the day, his assistants had signed up strangers to head petition drives in 28 states.

What began so innocently became the most formidable independent presidential candidacy in modern American history. Overnight, Ross Perot had been transformed into America's savior, someone who could cure the nation's problems with sound business sense and plain Texas talk.

The flood of calls did not end. Instead, they became a torrent. Perot's offices were a madhouse of ringing telephones and messages from people—eventually called The Volunteers—who wanted to help Perot's presidential bid.

To cope with the calls, Perot set up a phone bank of 30 lines on a rented floor in his office building. He called the new office the Perot Petition Committee. By the end of the month, the committee had 96 lines. And his volunteers needed more.

Perot struck a deal with the Home Shopping Network to lease 1,200 of their telephone lines. There were a quarter-million calls in a single day offering support for Perot. His office received one million calls in a 10-day stretch in March 1992.

With Perot in the race, the other political parties suffered. Polls taken at the Republican and Democratic primaries showed that Ross Perot, not Bill Clinton or George Bush, was the most popular candidate.

Perot was thrilled. He appeared on all the major TV talk shows. He spoke of spending $100 million or more of his own money on his campaign, causing his opponents to shudder. He went to rallies celebrating his name being placed on state ballots. It seemed all of America wanted Ross Perot for president.

Perot's strength was his use of TV and radio media. He refused to conduct a traditional campaign of traveling from city to city, making speeches, and having the press take his photograph. Instead, he held call-in shows, answering people's questions about what he would do as president.

Perot also refused to hire an army of advisors to tell him what to do and say. He surrounded himself with people he knew and trusted. His main advisor was long-time friend and lawyer, Tom Luce.

Luce was a smart and energetic. But he did not know how to turn an unmanaged all-volunteer campaign into something that would put Perot in the White House.

In March, Hamilton Jordan contacted Luce and offered his help. Jordan had been former president Jimmy Carter's White House chief of staff. Jordan was welcomed into the Perot camp and showed up at campaign meetings.

To cope with all the phone calls, Perot set up a bank of 30 phone lines in his office building. By the end of the month the committee had 96 phone lines.

He became Perot's campaign co-chairman with Ed Rollins, who had organized Ronald Reagan's 1984 landslide victory. Jordan handled the campaign and media strategies while Rollins handled the day-to-day operations. To help the campaign, Jordan and Rollins hired other professionals.

But soon Perot realized that the campaign professionals would not fit well with his simple, innocent approach to politics. A major issue between Perot and his co-chairmen was money and how it was spent. Perot had a distaste for spending his money on traditional campaign elements. He did not understand why he needed so many hired hands when he had The Volunteers. He considered the hirings wasteful.

Jordan and Hamilton proposed a $147 million campaign budget. Perot rejected it. He said he would never spend that kind of money on the campaign. Even more, meetings were shifted and cancelled. Memos went unread or unanswered. More and more, Perot was distanced himself from the hired professionals and their advice. His campaign began crumbling.

Pulling Out of the Race

To boost Perot's image, Jordan and Rollins bought a series of ads about Perot. Perot saw the ads—and hated them. He called the ads a waste of money, and they were never shown.

FULFILLING
OUR PRESENT

NASHVILLE CONVENTION CENTER

Perot made a speech at the NAACP convention where he referred to African-Americans as "you — your people." Many people were offended by Perot.

Perot was not having fun anymore. He was growing weary of the race, and it affected his campaign.

The final straw came on July 11 in Nashville, Tennessee. Perot made a speech at the National Association for the Advancement of Colored People (NAACP) convention. He referred to African-Americans as "you—your people." The press pounced on Perot. They did not like the way Perot talked down to blacks. As a result, Perot's popularity tumbled.

Perot decided to take charge of his campaign. He refused to be handled. It was his way, or no way.

Rollins had enough and resigned. Jordan thought about quitting also, but never had to make the decision. On July 16, a tired Ross Perot called a press conference and stated that he was out of a race he was never officially in. That left Democratic nominee Bill Clinton in control of the race.

Perot claimed he backed out for the good of the country. He did not think he could win the election. He thought his presence in the race would only disrupt its true outcome. He also did it for his family, whose lives were becoming disrupted.

Experts felt that Perot pulled out because he was never comfortable with the trials of a modern presidential campaign: the polls, the professional handlers, the advertising campaigns, and the tough campaign strategies. And he was certainly not used to being examined and criticized by the media.

Whatever the reason, Ross Perot was no longer a candidate. His decision disappointed some of The Volunteers—and crushed others. Many begged him to get back in, but their calls went unanswered.

No one was more disappointed than John J. Hooker. He couldn't believe Perot had backed out. The morning after the announcement, he called Perot and asked him to reconsider.

"Is there any possibility you would get back into it?" Hooker said.

"I'm still in the stadium," Perot replied. "I'm on the sidelines, I'm not in the game, but I am still here."

"Are you going to continue to be registered in all 50 states?" Hooker asked.

"Yes," Perot said.

"So if you're going to be registered in all 50 states, you're still in the stadium, then we'll see." Hooker hung up the phone, smiling. The first Perot campaign was over. But it looked like Perot would one day re-enter the game.

The Second Coming of Ross Perot

In the days that followed his withdrawal, Perot rebuilt his campaign from the top down—this time, the way he wanted it. Old volunteer leaders were replaced with the kind of white-shirt executives Perot liked. They were intelligent, but obedient, united, and quiet.

No professional handlers allowed, thank you. Tom Luce returned to his law firm, leaving Perot in charge of his own fate.

Perot's new organization was called "United We Stand, America." Its official mission was to get one of the remaining candidates to swallow Perot's tough solutions for America's ills. Unofficially, it was the second coming of Perot's campaign.

Through the late summer, Perot hinted at his return. The Democrats feared that a new Perot campaign would steal votes from Clinton. So they met with Perot in mid-September to talk him out of re-entering. Clinton sent Texas Senator Lloyd Bentsen to Dallas to talk to Perot.

"Ross," Bentsen said at the meeting, "we need to talk about your decision to get into this race."

"Yeah, OK," Perot replied.

"Quite honestly," Bentsen stated, "I don't believe you can win anymore. . . .You could endorse Bill Clinton. You could seal this election and make sure you and your people are seen as a part of the reason Clinton won."

"Those are all good points," Perot said. "Tell them to The Volunteers. They'll decide."

There was no mystery. Perot knew what The Volunteers would say. They wanted him for president, not Bill Clinton.

Three days later, Ross Perot made it official. He was back in the race. He had asked retired Vice Admiral James Stockdale to be his running mate.

Perot got back into the presidential race. He started
a committee called "United We Stand, America."
Its mission was to get the other
candidates talking about the issues.

*Presidential candidate Ross Perot speaks as
U.S. President George Bush and Democratic
candidate Gov. Bill Clinton listen during the
opening moments of the second presidential debate.*

With the election on November 3, Perot did not waste any time going on the attack. In the first two weeks of his return, he tried to recapture the magic and the fun that his first campaign had in its infancy.

Perot bought $24 million worth of TV spots. But these were not the usual 60-second TV commercials. They were 30-minute infomercials. Ross Perot was the star, and he filled each 30-minute spot with straight talk about the ailing economy. Armed with charts, graphs, and a pointer, Perot showed America what was wrong with the country and what he would do to fix it. His main topic was the federal deficit, for it was the greatest problem facing our nation.

Perot's ratings were amazing. Roughly 16 million people watched his first infomercial. His poll ratings inched upward.

Perot followed his infomercial success by winning the first presidential debate. Though many experts felt he could not win the election, it looked as though Perot would indeed affect the outcome. But then Stockdale stumbled in the vice-president debate, casting serious doubts on their chances. After the second presidential debate in Richmond, Virginia, the outcome seemed clear. Perot had no chance of winning.

In the end, Bill Clinton won the election with 44 percent of the popular vote. President Bush finished second with 38 percent. Ross Perot came in third with a surprising 19 percent.

"We'll Keep on Going"

Perot ended his campaign on a good note. He congratulated Bill Clinton as his followers booed loudly in the Dallas hotel ballroom where they all had gathered. "Wait a minute, wait a minute," Perot called out. "The only way we're going to make it work is to all team up together. Forget the election. It's all behind us."

For now, that is.

Perot's political future is not over. On election night, he told his supporters, "We'll keep on going as long as you want to keep going." With all his money and success, Perot's United We Stand, America might influence future elections and government policy. The organization will watch President Clinton's progress. If he stumbles, if the deficit grows and the economy does not improve, Ross Perot will be part of the 1996 election. He will be armed with more money, more followers, and the valuable experiences of 1992.

What We Learned from Ross Perot

Ross Perot affected many voters in 1992. His 19 percent of the popular vote made him the most successful independent presidential candidate since Theodore Roosevelt in 1912. He proved that independents could produce big, sweeping, and serious campaigns that could influence the overall outcome. All other independent candidates will be measured against his success.

Perot's 1992 presidential campaign also gave voters a glimpse of how future campaigns will be run. In his eight infomercials through October 26, Perot averaged 13 million viewers. In all but one case, his program did better than the network offering it replaced.

Most importantly, Perot's presence kept the 1992 presidential campaign on the issues. Perot forced the candidates to focus on the United States' problems and needs. The candidates who strayed from those issues were criticized.

As it turned out, the Democratic Party benefited from Ross Perot's campaign. Perot took many votes away from President Bush. Though Bill Clinton finished with less than half of the popular vote, it was enough to get him into the White House.

Perot's campaign ultimately showed how vulnerable and limited traditional politics could be in an angry time. The Democrats and Republicans learned that the political world is becoming tougher and more competitive. The voters—and Ross Perot—seem intent on keeping it that way.

Ross Perot with his family at the end of the 1992 presidential campaign. Ross may not have won the campaign but he made his point and he helped give a voice to many Americans.

GLOSSARY

Campaign—A series of actions a person undertakes to attain a political goal.

Debate—A formal discussion or argument.

Deficit—The amount by which a sum of money falls short of the required amount.

Democrat—A member of the Democratic Party.

Economy—The management of a country's resources.

Independent—A person not associated with any established political party.

Infomercial—A paid TV announcement that usually runs for 30 minutes.

Media—The means of mass communication, such as newspapers, magazines, radio, and television.

Mercenary—A professional soldier for hire.

National Debt—The total financial obligations of a national government.

Navigator—A crew member who pilots the course of a ship or aircraft.

Petition—A formal, written request.

Political Parties—Political organizations, such as the Democratic and Republican parties.

Primary—A meeting of registered voters of a political party for the purpose of nominating candidates.

INDEX